Facts About the Howler Komodo Dragon

By Lisa Strattin

© 2019 Lisa Strattin

FREE BOOK

FREE FOR ALL SUBSCRIBERS

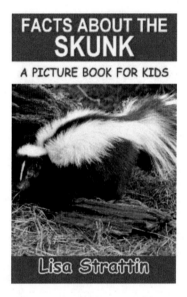

LisaStrattin.com/Subscribe-Here

BOX SET

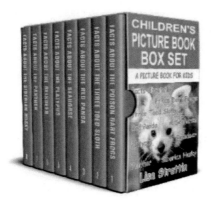

- **FACTS ABOUT THE POISON DART FROGS**
- **FACTS ABOUT THE THREE TOED SLOTH**
- **FACTS ABOUT THE RED PANDA**
- **FACTS ABOUT THE SEAHORSE**
- **FACTS ABOUT THE PLATYPUS**
- **FACTS ABOUT THE REINDEER**
- **FACTS ABOUT THE PANTHER**
- **FACTS ABOUT THE SIBERIAN HUSKY**

LisaStrattin.com/BookBundle

Facts for Kids Picture Books by Lisa Strattin

Little Blue Penguin, Vol 92

Chipmunk, Vol 5

Frilled Lizard, Vol 39

Blue and Gold Macaw, Vol 13

Poison Dart Frogs, Vol 50

Blue Tarantula, Vol 115

African Elephants, Vol 8

Amur Leopard, Vol 89

Sabre Tooth Tiger, Vol 167

Baboon, Vol 174

Sign Up for New Release Emails Here

LisaStrattin.com/subscribe-here

COVER IMAGE

ADDITIONAL IMAGES

Contents

INTRODUCTION

The Komodo Dragon is a large species of lizard that is only found on a few islands in the Indonesian archipelago region. They are actually a species of Monitor Lizard that has been evolving in isolation on these islands for years, which has led to it becoming very large.

The Komodo Dragon is not only the largest lizard in the world, but it also one of the most aggressive. They are so powerful that they are able to kill prey many times larger than themselves.

BEHAVIOR

They are solitary and powerful predators that roam a home range that is dependent on the individual lizard's size, with the average adult covering a distance of over 1 mile every day. They are also excellent swimmers, going from one island to another over a relatively long distance.

Although they are solitary animals, sometimes a group of them will come together around a single kill to eat. In order to catch the large animals they hunt, Komodo Dragons can sit for hours hidden in the waiting for an animal to pass by. They then ambush the victim with incredible speed and force.

APPEARANCE

These dragons have long, thick bodies, short, muscular legs and an awesome tail that is used for both fighting and for propping the animal up while standing on their hind legs. They have long and sharp, curved claws that are used for attacking and holding prey and for digging. Their greyish brown skin is covered in small scales and folds around their neck. They have small heads compared to their body size as well as wide jaws with a mouth filled with deadly bacteria.

Although the Komodo Dragons have good eyesight, they figure out what is in their surroundings by using their sense of smell. Interestingly, they smell with a long and deeply forked tongue. By flicking the tongue out of their mouth, the Komodo Dragon is able to "taste" scent particles in the air in order to locate both live and dead prey up to 5 miles away!

REPRODUCTION

Komodo Dragons can be seen in the company of one another during the breeding season. This is around the month of September, when males fight one another by standing on their hind legs, propped up by their tails as they try to win the right to breed with the females. After mating, the female lays up to 25 leathery eggs in a hole that she digs by herself into the soft sand.

The young will hatch after an incubation period that lasts for between 8 and 9 months and are completely independent from the mother when they leave their shell. Young dragons climb into the trees and stay there until they are big enough to hunt on the ground without being captured by many predators.

LIFE SPAN

Komodo Dragons tend to live for an average of 30 years in the wild.

SIZE

The Komodo Dragon is an enormous reptile that can grow up to 10 feet long and weigh over 300 pounds!

HABITAT

Today, they are confined to just five islands, which all lie in the Komodo National Park. The islands of Komodo, Rintja, Gillimontang, Padar and the western tip of Flores are the final remaining home areas for these huge animals. They are most commonly found in open woodlands as well as dry savannah and scrubby hillsides, and are also found to be found living around dried-up river beds.

They are becoming more threatened in their natural environments. This is due to deforestation, as man's timber operations have pushed the last of them into smaller and more isolated regions.

DIET

The Komodo Dragon is a meat-eating animal that only hunts and kills large animals to survive. Adults are able to kill prey much larger than themselves. many times they kill by ambushing their prey. In addition, they will follow any prey that gets away for miles until the prey eventually dies of blood-poisoning. This is caused by the bacteria in the Komodo Dragon's mouth that the animal sustains when the dragon bites into it!

Large mammals make up the bulk of the Komodo Dragon's diet including pigs, goats, deer and even horses and Water Buffalo. Young ones, however, prey on smaller animals in the trees such as snakes, lizards and birds.

The teeth of the Komodo Dragon are sharp and serrated, and the dragon cannot chew the food. Instead they tear pieces from the killed animal and throw it backwards into their mouths, swallowing it whole, using their neck muscles.

ENEMIES

Because they are the most dominant predator in their home environment, adults have no natural predators in their native areas. The smaller and vulnerable young however, have adapted to spending their early days in the trees to avoid being eaten by larger Komodo Dragons!

SUITABILITY AS PETS

It is not legal in many areas to keep a Komodo Dragon as a pet since they are protected as an Endangered Species. There are other logical reasons not to have one as a pet. For one thing, they are HUGE. Also, the bacteria in their mouths is poisonous. So, if you had one and the lizard was able to bite you, it would be dangerous for you.

You might be able to locate a zoo that has a habitat with Komodo Dragons for you to see. Just don't get too close!

COLOR ME

COLOR ME

COLOR ME

COLOR ME

COLOR ME

COLOR ME

COLOR ME

Please leave me a review here:

LisaStrattin.com/Review-Vol-281

For more Kindle Downloads Visit Lisa Strattin Author Page on Amazon Author Central

amazon.com/author/lisastrattin

To see upcoming titles, visit my website at LisaStrattin.com– most books available on Kindle!

LisaStrattin.com

FREE BOOK

FOR ALL SUBSCRIBERS – SIGN UP NOW

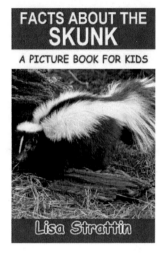

LisaStrattin.com/Subscribe-Here

LisaStrattin.com/Facebook

LisaStrattin.com/Youtube

Made in the USA
Monee, IL
16 October 2021